*Song X:
New and Selected Poems*

By Patrick Pritchett

Gnostic Frequencies
Salt, My Love
Antiphonal
Lives of the Poets
Burn – Doxology for Joan of Arc
Reside
Ark Dive

SONG X

New and Selected Poems

Patrick Pritchett

Talisman House, Publishers
Northfield, Massachusetts • 2014

Copyright © 2014 Patrick Pritchett
All rights reserved

No part of this book may be reproduced in any form or by any means, electronic or mechanical, including printing, photocopying, recording, or by any information storage or retrieval system, without permission in writing from the author and Talisman House, Publishers, LLC

11 12 13 7 6 5 4 3 2 1 Second Edition

ISBN: 978-1-58498-111-4

Acknowledgements: Some of these poems, nearly all since revised, first appeared in the following journals. My sincere thanks to the editors who first championed them. In particular, I would like to acknowledge my publishers for both their faith in my work and their commitment to the utopian ideals of the alternative, small press poetry community: Charles Smith (Arcturus Editions), the late Richard Wilmarth (Dead Metaphor Press), Charles Alexander (Chax), the late Anselm Hollo, Jane Dalrymple-Hollo, Laura Wright, and Mark DuCharme (Potato Clock Press), Bill Corbett (Pressed Wafer), Tod Thilleman (Spuyten Duyvil), and Ed Foster (Talisman House).

"The Lover's Dictionary" was published as a broadside by Ksenyia Thomas of Philadelphia. Michael Smoler produced a broadside of "Of The Thought that is Parousia" at Naropa's Kavayantra Press. "Salt, My Love" first appeared as a limited-edition artist's book from Chax Press, with hand-painted illustrations by Cynthia Miller.

*26, Angle, @ttached document, The Boulder Arts Paper, Colorado Review, The Common, Facture, For Immediate Release, Hambone, Interim, lower limit speech, LVNG, Mantis, Mirage Periodical #4, The Modern Review, New American Writing, New Review of Literature, Poetry South, Omnidawn Blog, Talisman, River City, Skanky Possum, Snout, Spoke, Square One, Ur*Vox*

for Ingrid Nelson

Contents

The Ark of Speech . . . 1

from *Reside* (1999)
    Autumn that is Burning . . . 4
    The Extraordinary Claims of the Personal . . . 6
    Assumption to a Jar of Light . . . 7
    Reside . . . 8
    Shelters of Form . . . 9
    Ark Dive . . . 11

from *Burn—Doxology for Joan of Arc* (2005)
    Prelude . . . 14
    Fable . . . 15
    Devotion . . . 17
    The Book . . . 18
    Whose Voice . . . 19
    Anneal . . . 20
    Canto . . . 22
    To Be Gone . . . 23
    The Master of Fire . . . 27
    The Falling (The Discontained) . . . 26
    Flue . . . 30
    "never the wholeness of her form" . . . 31
    Psalter . . . 32
    The Questions . . . 33
    Pyrelight . . . 34
    She Wanted . . . 36
    Glory of a Long Desire . . . 38
    Erased . . . 39
    Of Utterance . . . 40
    Of The Thought that is Parousia . . . 41
    To Remain in Love . . . 42

from *Lives of the Poets* (2007)
    English Lessons . . . 45
    Shelley Unbound . . . 46
    Intention Tremor . . . 48
    Beginning with a Line from Peter Riley . . . 49

from *Antiphonal* (2008)
    What the Psalmist Said . . . 51
    Homage to Samperi . . . 52
    For Reb Derissa . . . 54
    The Obscure Light of the Eye . . . 56
    Kerygma . . . 61

Salt, My Love, a ballad (2008) . . . 63

from *Gnostic Frequencies* (2012)
    Doctrines of the Lyric Body . . . 71
    Ariel on the Hope of Song . . . 73
    Ariel in the Marketplace . . . 75
    First Letter to Iamblichus . . . 76
    Ariel on Canopus & The Signature . . . 77
    Poem for Dismembering the Poem . . . 79
    The Spectral Logic of The Temporal Folds in on Itself . . . 80
    The Poem of Fire . . . 81
    To Be Two (Proleptic Seizure) . . . 82
    The Book of Drowning . . . 84
    Annals of the Tree of The House of Dust . . . 85
    Smoke's Book . . . 87
    Exact Presence . . . 88
    Archive . . . 90
    Etude for the Monstrance of Nothing . . . 91
    Summer in the Street of Cisterns . . . 93
    The Book of Remembering . . . 94
    Lyrics for the Lost Book of Ariel . . . 96
    The Dream of Yeats . . . 101
    H.D. in Egypt . . . 103
    Theurgical Etude for Nate Mackey . . . 104
    Thought's Smoke . . . 106
    Gnostic Frequencies . . . 108
    Tremble . . . 109
    In a Somer Seson . . . 110
    Envoi . . . 111

from *Song X*
    Ode to Song X . . . 113

Song X (on form) . . . 114
Summer as a Theory of Song X . . . 115
Number 9 Dream . . . 116
Aesthetic Theory . . . 117
Song X (neither dream nor actual) . . . 118
Dream of Song X . . . 119
Song X (final etude) . . . 121
Giving Account . . . 122
In Memory of My Nostalgia . . . 123
The Dream of Perfectible Capital . . . 125
Star dot Star . . . 126
Dianoia . . . 127
The Idea of Evening as Abode . . . 128
The Real Real . . . 130
The Lover's Dictionary . . . 131
Theory of Shelter . . . 132
Near Midnight . . . 133
Poem Beginning with a Line from Hugh Seidman . . . 135
Three Songs for the End of the World . . . 137
Heat Death . . . 139
The Idea of Limit (9/11) . . . 141
Coming of Age in the House of Dust . . . 143
the richness of my father at sea is a stone . . . 144
The Tears of Things . . . 145
Ballad . . . 147
Deixis . . . 149
The Empty Room . . . 150
Cadence . . . 151
The Ossuaries of Snow . . . 152
Grand Hotel Abyss . . . 153
Homage to the Raven . . . 155
Six Gnostic Songs . . . 157
The Death of the Author . . . 161
The Dream of the Poem . . . 162
Dante or, The End of Poetry . . . 163

That the body of light come forth
                from the body of fire

    — Ezra Pound

Go write yourself a book and put
therein first things that might define a world

           — Robert Duncan

Or maybe this
is the sacred

           — Michael Palmer

The Ark of Speech
        (after Jean-Louis Chretien)
           for Ingrid Nelson

Of making many books there is no end,
yes nor an arrival ever before the single
page that will pronounce us as
we are speechless.

For whoever keens to the sound of boats on water
moved by their dissolving tunes
agrees to be frayed by catastrophe
plunged to the neck in the blue moon's gold.

It is by the singular instance of not knowing
but folding up inside the rebel angel's cause
that we enter a second life.
Its ministry for damnation. Its syllabaries of pleasure.

When you smile you say the wonder
of the lit world is all in the small letters
of its more intricate knowings.
As could shower us with *caritas,* seeds for

the dream of seeing how the ark of speech
shelters more deeply than we could guess.
Or that in our praying here, together, such desire
as would risk it all is set

cool against the continual *mysterium*
that is both pulse and semblance
of the glory that is mereness.
To speak of the book is to speak of the world.

Is to sit here speaking across this table to you
and burn to the edge the words for the poem
that source the flesh into
its acts of beauty.

It is to speak presence as the bevel of the wind
speaks light across the face. Willing the hour
into the stunned posture of our séance.
Or does beauty have the power to send us further?

from *Reside*

Autumn that is Burning
      for Jorie Graham

Directly there is a fire we say autumn,
as though burning
were the only word
to pronounce this wind
at our throats,
its coolness.

In the beginning of autumn is a field
of thinking about autumn.
About the fall and the desire
of things to fall
and the desire of things to
be many and not one.

The description of autumn begins
with an appeal.
The ineffable longing
of the body to be torn to pieces,
to be scattered directly
there is a fire

in what we say is autumn.
By location mean locution.
A singularity. A stillness.
A quality of insuperable being
that is also and always
the most continual diminishment.

So that: the border of autumn and its recessions are one.

Or else two always in their going,
feather to fire and smoke to harbor.

Say that the Broken Boat
is yet another name for autumn,
for that which is best viewed at twilight,
in a period of general weariness,
as a series of descriptions
made from wood
and aptly entitled "autumn."

    Blue wood.
    Wood that burns.

The Extraordinary Claims of the Personal

In the little room we placed the objects of the little room. So that belonging, its assurances, its meters, could reside, could be said "to glow."

This is where the earth turns, in its oiled chambers, on the weary spindle of its naive lathe. The core of earth is ferrous, under pressure.

Which is prime. Which is oceanic. The sudden warming that leads to turbulence (in belted layers). The forecast of the future reassured by the promise of chaos, disruption. The two or three words that wound, always, as way to verify the extraordinary claims of the personal.

The word "rain," for instance.
The word "signal."
Its imputed privilege.
Its desire for enclosure.

To prepare the little room and say, this is where the living accrues, this is where it takes place.

Or say: this is the story I am meaning to tell, the story of elision and forgetfulness. The story of a collision and the subsequent version known as The Embracing.

To tell a story is to wander off the point. Is to make atonement for forgetting.

We were water, once, we said, "Water us." We were money, we yearned for it
and prayed, "Spend us." We were slippage, we said, "Desire us."

And — sotto voce — "Burn us."

Assumption to a Jar of Light

By whom we receive
tincture
of salt, the red weed
of bread,
and a bed to lie on,

Alive, as a jar of fire
lit by sky,
by the assumption of
light to a place
where Lazarus walked,
eating dust,

Mandate crossing boundaries,
octaves,
humming vatic tunes
as who would be the keeper
of the syllabary,
its mutenesses.

To be torqued by erasure
into flame,
into resting.
Light there.
Standing on the old rules.

Reside

Instead of disaster
this motion
across a page
a sign of breathing
in which
everything becomes
possible.

I mean the words.
The stand of them.

As a swan
in the rookeries of ice
evolves a science
of lift-off.

Not
the name circling its own
cleft dimension.

But what issues.

What resides.

The beauty of the novices out gathering
sugar for the fire of their lives.

Shelters of Form

lower-octave-register

Here it is nothing but the sun and the tropes of enclosure.
We daunt the window, the sweetness of its
mitre and withdraw to the land of the spoon.
Such honey as lives among us.

october-stare-to-harbor

Where the street is also a form of fugue & following a line
means entering the paraclete in the rosebush.

A leaf descends, decants a landing.

Blown across a world, it resembles joy.

dross-measure-lathe

Then agile, we turn to gold, all stammers.
The synapse of a late afternoon breeze
set to a tune of palace and decay.

Clearly, you were made to be its rib.

shelter-migrant-form

How is it it happens? I am low to the field, standing
derelict. A dialect of weather, its most intimate repetitions.

    There is a longing to make many lists.

But between a wish and the rain is a longing to be overwhelmed.

caesura

A blue stone receives its light, a sieve
sundered in the middle.
In the middle of a stroke gone wide.
By a cup of water such catastrophes as home.
Signaling shelter, but breaking form.

Ark Dive
        i.m. Ronald Johnson

In ark-dive,
grey encomium.
Grey imperium of
the all-day rust-dawn
-ed day.
If amen, then a willow
& its sibilance too.
Or water bluster
in stone-cracked creek.
Force of lone stone empty
on an earth swept
wide.
And stricken by
late winter-sun-and-lance.
By this tide, great gong:
ever-and-a-going,
gone.
We go so — in measure-
less tread, dividing
song from wing.
Particle-cleave, *(parousia)*
your run is ended.
A nascent valence
resumes.
Foremost among foot-
falls and sober
in Elysium to be going
if light there is ever sober
or windonsea any-
thing *but claritas,*
supra urbem, supra sapientia,
bells building spire

on spire in the true
font of soul's un-
encrypted in-
scription.

>	(Hover a while.
>	Breathe this and be glad
>	of it.

from *Burn*

Prelude

It is by a passage of heat/she makes
the entrance from one body to another.
A presage then, a long coat of heat,
worn so that the body's uncertain arithmetic
disappears into its folds,
providing a kind of sublunary light,
a replenishment beneath the uneven pressures
of the half-white moon.

The body is Aleph. Omega burns
in the space where angels paint
their halos, painful as tattoos.
A halo is a warble of the body,
an exhalation of heated particles,
an instruction to the light
adorning the inner walls of cells.
The trailing edge of the body
leads to the touch of fire.

Who dreams of fire dreams
the imperishable body.
In the colony of the body
an hour of hair lit by the sun
is a fountain pouring,
a river knitting
the interstices
of first this text, then that.
Read it in the spiral glyphs of a spent match.

    Unseal the book.
    Sink the raft.

Fable

Joan, dear Joan,
the night
is a planet on fire
saying: the question can burn the asker.

Do you assent
to be consumed?
        To be the bone of charity
fumed
        to a banner of smoke?

Or submit to
        halo
        ("and crown of me go fast to death")

Be lathed
till you glow like
a wound
Beyond
annunciation's clamor of

Wings?

o Voice descanting
(skewered on a stamen)
a constellation of bees or
hyacinths/ trembling

And in the
crushed air
        you agreed:
to be the Bride
stripped

down to
the bone
of speech

Devotion

And in the longness of this light

I have made exhibition

not to be endured but

as the sequence of a few rounded things

the sputter of green

in its woundingness of green

for which the word for green is impassable

in the dumb canticle of its saying

the sonogrammic hand shines revealed

in the basement of the face

the skull inhabited of wine

& shorn of wing to be broke

on the pavement that is west

display the bones murmuring from their escarpment

encrypting the body of dust in the body of flame

The Book

To write my name
in the Book of Fire.
Where every page is bent
between song and smoke.
(To enter it in tears).

From stillness comes a listening.
From listening the things beyond naming.

So soul drifts through body
like white fog through
bare branches?

The pages of the body
will be initialed in flame:

      hair
      hands
      ribs
      knees

      Mouth

Whose Voice
      for Kathryn Bigelow

That the true burning was for the voice.

In the cloth of her own.

No radiant tyrannical Other.

The secret of the voice is not to name the end.

And ascend by way of perpetual utterance.

To say *woman* in the court of kings without kneeling.

And inhabit the space where the Lord is the Fold of the Mother.

And to scratch your name into paper with ink.

The AutoGraphic gesture of becoming.

As a warlord would do it, mastering techne.

All the self contained inside a Sign.

And then to erase it.

Anneal

That I am annealed, by a kind of praise,
and fall & kneel
to the ground & its sores
& kingdom.

That I should do so
by the name I have
made for the living
& in the flare of what
takes *au-dela*
this imperfect verb
of being.
                That I
should care to fall
all the way
        down.

That this body is
the rufous cataract of
its own stunning
instrument
and
a power of dust
to collide
with unknowing.

That *abba* is my word
for Fire,
though it flay me
on the naked face of Noon.

Where I am forever
shed of this rain, its poverty,

orphaned
into nomination
beyond all care.

Canto

Govern this star
by a muteness as white
as the pleasured
annals of love
the commingling, the slippage
(the porousness)
be all my private
mutations enacted

recognize this
for you are estranged
by lake & by book
where we walked
where we clung
of the Looking
inside a startled O
wave, my wood
casting the long court
of days

flicker, emptiness
fire sent down
to earth
on the skin of
the narrow, the human

To Be Gone

Instead of "grace"
this wholly confused sense
of an overwhelming whiteness to things
the vantage point of obscure campaigns: belltowers and moons
occluded by an oracular glow
        dispensing
        dumb beatitudes

As what is white
could be the blue burn of snow,
its underwater songs the haunts & valves
where the beautiful might be encrypted in glass, bane & boon
to the ingress of Christ and his windhover rhythms
        tune
        of the true monster

Who loves you
and abides beside you, a blade of grass spelling
sorrow in runes that are a cost to the beholder & derange
the canticle of thrones with the black wave of a dune
no man knows the motions of the gone season
        the figures
        of lapsed gold

Arcs a breach
from all our days, sundering ship from earth
farness from ache, the weather of insane echo
from the touch of dwelling and the tissues of last tunes:
kissed arch and running tide and ruined radiance
        of lips, eyes,
            posture, bloom

The Master of Fire
>for Lisa Jarnot

The Master of Fire, he spoke to me, he said: *the wheel and what it moves grow old inside the flame.*

He said: what is essential to the heart is Heat.

And she motioned with her hand to follow her into the canyon of trees. They were all of flame. No burning there, but the clear light of oxygen devouring the lungs.

A river giving off smoke; it was sweet.

The Master of Tongues moved through the shadows of flames. She was battlement and estucheon. The myriad grooves of war worshipped in her wake.

"Mistress," I said, "men are slow to move. By what agency may I touch them?"

He spoke, he said (cutting me): *in no way does a rose issue but by the water at its feet and from the tongues of tiny flame and out of the abandon of the West and the names of the Invisible, that are written where only the Dead may read them.*

And she showed me the graves of the angels that are spinning motes of ice around a ruby sun.

to sleep, She said, *is to make a bargain with the dust.*

And: *the catastrophe of living is boon to Man.*

She said: *the supernatural, a means for constructing realism.*

The Master of My Voice entered the tree of my thought, as a bird all on fire, but the fire was blue and slowly turning in the night.

It spoke to the stream. It said: *That boundaries exist, that edges occur, is an Overcoming and a Sorrow. Movement decrees loss. An edge is to approach. The temple was hallowed by a series of desecrations. An object is an object when the eye refuses the Other. To hold a Face is to regard.*

Thus spoke the Mistress of All Lies. Her armor was a kite, her tongue a ribbon of blood. Old Bone of Dawn moaning in the wind & nothing in his eyes. Nothing at all.

The Falling (The Discontained)

i.

What if this language
were *the* language, *the* closeness itself,
closer, closest to the heart?
And would you then?
Exalt me?
Would you then?
Pour forth?
In a heartbeat.
(Reservoir).
I ache to
contain the simple drop of
the cruet.
Deep in shadow,
in ageless alcove.
Above the hood of flesh.
Above the hood of skin.
Those eyes.
And in this hand the skin.
And in this heart the road.
To travel just one grain of.
That is all.
The heart asks.
And I am just now by.
Your brightness lit, dis-
contained.
Your calamity of light.
Falling. Fallen.
Glowing all around.
All around me.
Brightness?
Discontained.

ii.

And now by light
I move in circles

And move in circles
& tell my wine

the story of my voice
that is my voice

the story of my circling.
How I am contained.

narrow are the vessels

Narrow the sun running long leg
in stride of stream,
in clearing of stream singing

golden with the light of fawn.

Telling me the infinite doxology.
Telling me its damage across the fields.
Telling me I must remember.

That is a Claim, the dearest.

Folded into
the smallness of my circle
moving as my voice
moves
and the world made even larger.

iii.

Because rain blurs the windows
till the blur is all translucence.

Because days when the day is so long
it falls of its own weight.

And I am falling as I am falling
for I am claimed by an unattaining.

Because a moment that is not a touching
of the water where geese float, more serene than the Dauphin's barge

that cuts a path of ripples into sunset's glass.

Its image unbroken. And I can't
I can't even add one plus one.

Because the numbers
are grown old, the numbers

because it's your eyes.
The wave pulling the chain

pulling it up. And from moon, from ocean
it is golden, this delight. It is glowing

and I am old among all
the leaves you scatter Shatter

on the path
to an unbecoming.

iv.

And the Beauty of this world makes me sick:

For instance, *your eyen two wol.*

For instance, a crease of dusk where neck meets jaw.

For instance, vortical energies, arms & legs akimbo.

For instance, the sun of youth. (Blind, blind, blind).

For instance, the inadmissible, the staggering load of.

For instance, the capering in the neutral middle, but nowhere else.

For instance, the unhappy genius of the heart.

For what it cannot.

For what is not.

For what?

Flue

That the angel is a bursting.

And a form of growing godness or decay.

That it is inside & also not.

That I am the bucket lowered & re-lowered.

That what becomes me

is more than   that

To be this sharpness turning in your hand.

And then, to be this wind.

Beast lacquered in the gold of its seraphic tongue.

The description of the godly speeding up the flue of bones

"never the wholeness of her form"

I have to go away.
And never come back.
Inside a cup,
or a piece of cloth.
Like a star
blown off course.
A wind
lovely
with the cause of
its dash & aftermath.
To be called
is to be split apart
is to set foot
on the causeway
of wound
and small shelter.
No
water or bread.
Carried
only by
longing.
Enduring inside
the pause.
Where breathing must be more.
And multiplied by and.

    the gone into the

Psalter

My psalter
made of dust.
Made under
wingtip's brush.

By your caress I feel my folly,
even to the Seventh Dwelling Place,
where the heart is split
unnaturally into horizon

& on the Chair of Merkabah
I am kept alive,
& turning
O turning.

By this I am given
to speak to you.
Who press the candle
of the body to the gift of wood.

Usher the name of dream
by which sight is riven.

The Questions

Asked if:
the numinous sorrow of sparrows
was a voice in the vesicle of her head.

Asked if:
ply on ply the strand of grain
and its hour was a dryness and a comfort and a kindling.

Asked if:
whether the longing for the Other
were not the disease God planted.

Asked if:
the brightness was the Sign of Presence,
its manifold pressures & heats.

Asked if:
the music at noon could hold the font
where roses bled, monstrous.

Asked if:
a Season were a Mote, and if that Mote
were wholly sourced by the tune & fall of its noise.

Asked if:
the gravity of these burdens, their plutonic weight,
held the task of breathing what other air.

Pyrelight

But say there is a Light
a light   in the heart of oak

Say it is the armor of   the Saint
who burned in her   wood

Its visions   Under the catafalque
of Spring which held   the dying

flowers to the light
all the dying of the   snow

figured there Say
it was a heart

and that it glowed
perdurable   above the Sonnets

And the lake whose escuchteon
was a lily   the lily

Whose crown was   a fly
the Black tear   like oil

That struck the dust
of Golgotha

the Arch
of the ruined   Amenities

of Water
of Superfluities

But in the wood of   the oak
in its cells   a Light

a wind

Then the roaring
Sight

She Wanted
        for Jay Cocks

blue blister of Sky
            split open,
cascade & diadem of unthinkable
rooflight   Wanted

spire on spire
        and a little bread,
the golden letters in the book
of Jeremiah.

Water wheel
        all day all night
and no song but
        bells.

Dilation & loveliest of fevers.
Holding empire sway.
The name that was not
        forthcoming.
Neither Jehanne nor Pucelle. A moment off
sunstruck walls in Chinon.

Yes,
to put off her clothes. Attire
        entirely
in the voice of Glory.

                To fold,
to close, to crease & clutch
the gap
        of bitter breath
with uttered

spark.   Wanted this.
          Soar
to fever, yet poor.

Glory of a Long Desire

To go
past nocturne
as if blue were the road

Sunset
the vowel inside the body's veins

Body
the water you navigate
to come to the harbor
of body

"Solely the death of the body
authorizes the journeying practice
which is speech."

                    The bell is a wave
it speaks
        of prayer
the dream
before the war
when Fire was the word
for a signature beyond naming

No branch in the world for the sign of this stillness.
It's by means of the impossible that
speech erases speech

Erased

[That ash would   ]
[singe & marrow   ]
[hidden in   the angel]
[a face] [smoke as   air]

[coronal   ] [noon   ]

[the real   ] [itself the   ]
[flurry of   ]
[seeking a refuge]

[be   trestle to] [whatever   creased]
[Morning] [   ] [   ] [and stunned]

[agate] [last] [   ] [sun]

- 39 -

Of Utterance

Because the pressure of rain on the skin
is like a natal wound.

Because the drift of cloud through pass
sets the field to green fire, its branches.

Because I hurry to the wing of the limb
where the blue wheel and its flickering discharge certain energies.

Because the water. Because the stillness.
What is raised to the lips drowns.

The life of action set to another music.
Because the sun is the respirator of the afterlife.

The shimmer of its light across the grove of trees
burns the master's eyes.

Rectitude. Stone of the muse at the bottom of .
Enunciating "flame."

Because a cicatrix forms over every word
and we call it utterance.

Of the Thought That is Parousia

What song of the lord pursues   What song
what moan of the earth moves to
a day   A day is supine   It lies before
sun   What sun is this   My love by
window is a movement of water
Is a movement of water under light
And what light to speak   Or am I
moving   Under sign of wood to speak
it is love this morning   To the purse
of gold and for a song the lord will
Be or Is Bright Now   To make of it
a gift   Make of the sun caress or O

      we / shadow / home

To Remain in Love
          after Messiaen

The sign of your care
will be this smoke
as it drifts past
the window. Will be
this field in a stance
of green,
the fold of it
both wave
& particle,
hold and flow.

To make music from
an easter of starlings
on the grass,
knowing what we
know about
the structures
of loss.
The ache inside
the wine.
Or we will write
the larger account
of it as people
in love with dust
etch the sayings
of dust
on the glass.

The sun is occluded
under the wobble of forecast.
The space of
our holding here
keeps a measure

with the pace
of its dissolve.
Justice.
What equals the will to love.
Agency of a leaf
blown against a wall.
Agency of a wall
thinned to a grain
of smoke.

from *Lives of the Poets*

English Lessons

I arrived at the university in the fall of the year
having _____ at X (dormition) (reboot).

To build the single letter would be the difficult task.
Requirements to follow.

It was spring in spite of what I said and the blowing of a horn
over water, over light held us in its grip.

By that I mean I was alone.

In the long evenings we traveled to the lake
having been given wine and instructions
for aligning the pages of the dead.

      Who are the dead, you asked.

All those who never said
in life and now want to

      enter the word
                and be stilled.

On such a dipsalmic afternoon
the bitterness of long study
is like the parable of the rabbi
and his plate of bones.

      Who goes to the book without hope
      of the ghost.

I mean the way water quivers under light.

Shelley Unbound
        for Jeffrey Robinson

We have journeyed toward the beyond
        which is an atmosphere all its own.
            Made of vibrations or particles
    and the forgiveness of that debt
              that is a kind of ruined arch
                besides which sits a blonde woman.
   She knows our names
        & all our abysses
     and who lives in our houses
and she says that the things we give off
must be electric.

       Everything that shines
with its own light
      subjoins us to some hour when
         the city goes all blue
         and
   what I know of the sea is not scraps and patches
     but this endless talking
        in which I shall meet you
   like a wild swan
     shivering in the wideness of
          exertion.

But the vanished world looks back at us
      and we grow smaller.
    There is a castle and then
           a gulf
  and we know we cannot yet come home.
       To think of the boundary without thinking
         of touch?
   When your write you send account

                    of rains and the number of crowns
                        and the boat of the actual
                              that is passing continually.
            For a word is a species of enclosure. The iron bar
and residence of a thousand forms all arriving
                        on the same day.
     Justice is nothing unless it is first
a beautiful translation.

Intention Tremor
      i.m. Ric Caddel

In the dark, you sd.
Where the great names of light are built.
      Light, yes.
      As a gull's wing
      slices then closes
grey morning.
Invisible scar of supra-legium.
      Supernal book inflamed
      of days.

& we are so upon this turf as members
of that house that prays its praise
      as a stumbling
over words.
Their sweetness our ruin.
As in reaching forward to grasp at one
      the slip occurs
      must always occur.

They come to cover us now
in the deepness of their holding.
Make the bourne of
intention tremor
run smooth.
If ever a word could speak & not burn us
      with its waver.
      Insubstantial
gleaning of the fold that falls
      foaling, foliate,
all round us, so.

Beginning with a Line from Peter Riley

This is where love fastens us to the earth, undoing us, as dust, the long fade to anonymity, to every evening in which the only thing that matters is not the end of day, but the absolution given to beginnings.

Because living is impure light, stolen from a darkness that surrounds it, & what is lost in the separation haunts us with the promise of another disaster – the true boon of the soul sheathed in white fire.

In the mute globe of breath that is the heart lallalation trembles. Echoing to subsidence on a gray shore.

Threshed from the pulp of matter the sublime arcs to senescence. Planet-fall in the grinding hour of prayer. Ardent or faltering, a face shines from a grainy photo. The yellowed ivories, the smoothed woods, bend the room toward lateness. Listless.

The history of helplessness is the wish for lyric.

from *Antiphonal*

What the Psalmist Said
      i.m. Robert Creeley

To go spoken, surely,
craving what is silent there
and neither wholly known
nor unbroken, as of
cadences, a mindfulness,
a kind of midrash even,
the story of a bone
and what is found there
a crystal dust, adjunct
to the speck of flame
and in the world
to partake of it, as
the eye partakes, make
a decent economy,
what is scriptural
is always this sense of loss.
The outgoing.
The distance inside
the *pater noster*
of a single syllable.

Homage to Samperi

       1.

Now they wood the bright
they river the great house
launch the body of incontestable
light.

XPISTOS
harbinger
daily the
wing-run.

2.

The ontological is a proposition.
       What, it asks,
does the beautiful
            carry?

3.

System restore?

      The grain of the real says the new
      by not consuming it. Past clarity & more than
      surplus it subsumes the ache at the center
      the soaked kernel by which finitude
      scrapes the sign for Sunday onto our knees.
      A single kiss darkens everything.

4.

It is
not this day
its wind
hover
motion
its stillness
inside tree
vein
its
standing
wave
but more
uncertain
still
the knowledge
of nocturne
at noon
attesting
the lesions
of song.
The raggedy
body
asleep in
sunlight
dreams
the aesthetic
a sphere of
poverty
mitred
with birdsong.
To remedy loss
forsake the known.
The soul
is a speck
of pollen.

For Reb Derissa

To throw into this earth the most beautiful flowers
and say, with the Masters,
      Neshamah, Eyn Sof—the snow is falling.

     When the Baal Shem Tov, He of the Good Word
walked through the woods
        each word he spoke
    was as *kavana* — a lifting inside of
           mystery
       for those who are fallen
a speaking to sparks asleep inside signs, their obdurate
      husks gleaming with fire
          inside the abyss
       we walk through.

He said: "Song
shifts the lonely.
    Merges their
letters into the
sphere of
    longing."

He said: "Whoever prays and sings, eats and speaks
      reads, reads all the time
touches the fallen, the sparks of
    a letter, the first letter
where it sleeps in the dust murmuring
     of what is to come."

He said: "Everything is still waiting to be said."

And he urged us to remember:
"all names drift west, all names are a series of

lapses & scissions. What I will call
nevertheless, hope."

As the word for in the beginning
is also covenant of fire.

As Elohim may also mean
burn this wood, dissolve its bright vowels.

Obscure Light of the Eye
      for Karen Jacobs

i.

Eye
is the field of it
the overarching that astonishes
the body with the shadow of a depth
or its simple migratory prism
the showing of the slow dust of
transfiguration
held to flame of air
to the wideness of river
the complex host
of separation and desire.

           In the eye
           the beam is a latticework
           net of receptors
           the distant made immediate
           the near an intimate room
           breath the issue of a touch
           grazed by
           the web of belonging
           the fineness of the instant
           that is also the longitude
           of our desertion.

ii.

It is the myth of light
ascendant the crux
of jubilation that makes
possible a world and its forms
of speech the saying
of the obscure light
by which we love one
another through the reciprocal
modes of brilliance
and penumbra
signifying totality
the feeling of
crossing the street
at midnight the entrance
to the grove or sweep
of grass the sense of
being amid
in this blaze of care
where the iron world stuns
us poor along the axis
of diurnal bone.

> Eye to eye
> and speech from
> speech rising
> in the morning of the room
> of the visible
> the stone surrounded
> by what halo
> what shadow
> even the unspecific bird
> on its unruined winter branch
> would drink from it

        for light has turned it
        to water
        and water has knelt
        before the eye
        proclaiming the kingdom
        of sight.

iii.

But who looks plummets to accord.
The inlet and perverse obligation of the Thing
shining in its thingness and then.
The sense that we must persevere in our looking.
Staring stone-straight-to-sun and ardent
with the hope of a greater burning.
That would lift or erase, sever or join, the totality
of all possible perceptions.
Who we might become in the instant
of the gaze and its consumption
its self-emptying gesture to the abyss of
a single day that contains us and.

Boon of sundering.
The faraway is what exaggerates me.
Size of a rolling point of an object in space because it surpasses me
blesses me.
Withdrawal of domain.
You claim the world as the very first
and are undone in the mode of the body of another uninhabited
but for the liquidity of this exact
circumambient stammer and blush.
This preposterous wideness of O.

iv.

And when I say that I see something at a distance
I mean the express size and approach
and I mean the rise of a greater convergence
and I mean the things of this world are braided with light
and falling and I mean
my body is broken open
and the stones and the stars are inside it.

v.

To the wavering tune of the visible
the heart of the world scatters in the prime
moment of its opening.
Soaring where I am touched and touching
this incomparable sonorous being overwelling
the order of the seen
to repeat the interweaving circle
of vision, fission and return.

vi.

That there is vision.
        That the eye is aperture and conduit.
That it sinks and is subsumed
        in the flesh of the world the carnal
realm emitting photons before
        a theater of clouds
the obscure lamp
        doubling us in our beauty and decay.
Immense air alone burning
        in its nothingness.
What holds us to horizon in the dream of being
        able to go beyond.

Kerygma
        for Anne Waldman

      Who sings
beyond the genius of
        I mean the body,
its voice ghosting
movements
of a larger shore

wave, lap, dis-
solve roar

Who said
the prayer is nothing
but words assuming the shape
of smoke

The work of fire,
like the work of night,
where the saying of the sacred
is a message about
the Impossible

Push of the dream:
        where what gets said
        is always the longing to
        say more.

Salt, My Love (a ballad)

Salt, My Love – A Ballad

>for Ingrid, who wrote,"At last the light dims, and salt finds our mouths again."

     1.
So a tree waves in the wind
and what my best life aspires
to when it aspires
is to complete a form.
Any form is perfect if you say so.
If you say form, if you say
that form is the love
of silence and
the speaking of silence
into form's hollow,
then hold me, as form
makes of it a body
and always we are there,
two brightnesses aloft,
two bodies in the wash
of salt and shadow, shadow
and a stray bit of sun.
And we are found again
there on that same shore
(it is like your bed)
as waking again means
touching you again
and I am held low over you
and you hover in, above me,
and however I am washed
means the salt is taking us
both out to sea.

2.

What desires us. Desire?
What includes us in desire?
The sky, no – then the moon?
The moon is ice, or maybe particle,
or else grain of sight at night,
its cloud in the eye, its shadow
like a cluster of clouds
and what are they saying tonight
about love?
I don't know, I can't hear them,
but they are smiling as they say it
and I think I know it means something
about two people
and two people who are
about to kiss.

3.

Ballad means community. The communal. Its desire.
The desire of coming before the other.
The way of speaking another way of speaking.
That is the other.
That is you.
You are the ballad.
Ballad as a mode of staying communal in your saying
meaning we have found a way of saying together.

That is lovely.

4.

Then I am beginning here.
As someone who is learning how to say
the things of beginning that are also
the things we belong to
for a long time to follow
as they are the things that are
initial – initializing – a form
of striking fire, say,
from out of one another's skin.
Or of saying, simply, I am
here – I am here now.
And here you are, too.
We will be very pleased
to take each other as we are
and no other.

5.

So the longing for the ballad
is a longing for a shard.
Steadfast. Obdurate.
A star shines down.
A high star winds us in its light
like a bed made all of white.
Like that high ancient bed
wherein we say Amen.
Amen, and kiss me, love.
Kiss me with your kiss of whiteness.
Your ballad that is your body
saying all its perfect form.

6.

But there are things.
What about the things?
Who speaks for them?
Or do they speak themselves
and then what?

The things are integral
to the ballad mode because
like words the things are
what say us and not
the other way around.
I have brought some things
and others I have left behind.
Some there are that have left me, too.
Some things I have
and do not want:
Frigidaire, for instance.
And sodas.
And the other, troubling
things that I will not name here.

But to want "successive happenings"? (Yes).
Or else to be the instrument
for their expression? (Yes, again, yes).
As a thing is what says the word
that we become when we are out
walking and naming the world that
returns in our names for it, but returns
otherwise, too.
As you are a naming of me
from outside any point I can quite see
and to be so named by you is very pleasing.
It is like a ballad.
It is made of the archaic

that persists in other names, other modes.
It is what is singing still
inside the lyric when the lyric
is all but finished and.

    7.

Modulate this loom. Stroke its body with the grain.
He said: your body in the sun. Yes.
Your body in the sun, but
also your body as you speak to me, as you gaze
at me so solemnly I swear I never know
what you are thinking but to be held
that way, to be held
in such regard is something
I cherish even as I cannot
find but must let slip away
any word for it I thought
to have mastered.
I have mastered nothing.
But I am floating here with you,
you are under me, I am inside of you.
Is this the ballad yet?
If it is a ballad it is better
than any song David ever crooned.

    8.

It seems I am some other in a ballad
no one has yet said.
Or that you are the ballad
in the very mention of you.
Your otherness.
Crowning me with its sweat. Your sweat.

You are someone who comes
from a long line of pronouncing
the things as they are with such care.

9.

The vibration of a word set us going.
That could be like a ballad, long-resonant.
That day in the coffee shop. That day on the hill.
That night where you first kissed me
and I lost all my words.
But they found me again.
They, and the things they named.
All the ballads for your name.
Who wrote them? Who is still writing them?
What are we to do about them
and who will sing them?
Who will sing them in the long posture
of their glowing, in the long evening
of what they are thinking to say
as someone is saying them?

10.

Salt, my love.
Salt for the dove's kingdom.
Salt for the kingdom of a dove
or else a porch where we met a cat
and it was a cat who cared to follow you.
Salt for the words that are things
and the words for saying things.
The things that say us back to us as us.
As we are standing here, in the minor radiance of salt.

Its aftermath.
Its lozenge and all its grain
dissolving on your bed of whiteness,
your bed of floating.
The floating that is annihilation.

That is salt, my love.
Salt of all our rooms and days.
The salt that is also all our talking.
The sweetness and greatness of talking with you.
The talking that goes on inside
and through us.
A constellation, linked by word,
by touch, by
O.

O ballad, you are salt, my love.
Saying this. Then saying that.
Saying ballad.

Saying any form is perfect if you say so.

from *Gnostic Frequencies*

Doctrines of the Lyric Body

First of all, it is whisper, rather than
light. A torched sibilance in the ear
a refrain not a shine, the earth
heathen with the tombs of
sacre coeur, their dismal fonts
their baptismal flights.

Absent music, language is
catastrophe.
Mere prose is grief before
the torn rose, the grain
of wood insane inside
the book's crooked pages.

Whatever is read there
is abandoned to trance
to the flowering silence
that folds the sign
engathering the sink
& pith of matter.

Resonant crystal directing
signals over impossible
distance. The Cloud
of song/the light tree
nested in stanzas of *shantih*
or whiteness, or candor.

Let the sinking of form
also be form — the mystery of
insatiate skin glowing with
the tendon of flame &
the story of its leaping over.

The shape of two crows, cruciform, in

the boat of their going over.
Beautiful, we say, a wing is destroyed
in its motion. But moving always.
As séance through scroll.
Bright amid the flare
of the letter, its folding.

Garment me, love, with the mere scrap of. Shadow.

Ariel on the Hope of Song

      For the skull
is like a diamond, pierced
        with light and withholding it.
                Of its many griefs
Ariel says we must insist on a mode more extravagant
        than song
            but still issued in a form
by which the notes will hold
the tone.

Not mourning, she writes.
        (The entry is from the Fourth Ennead).
           Elegy, she seems to feel
      is too blunt an instrument.
                Because the radiance of the dead
is transferred by fire
        and there we may read (or so she suggests)
            the aurugenic properties of a midnight
                luminous without religion.

Then too
the doctrine of the subtle body maintains
        that passion is best treated as a propagation
      of waves.
           Ekstasis sounding
           through specific harmonies
                whose resonance
           at twilight
           signifies the dyad's perforation
           and the gift of oil to the tree.
Made from tears, ascendant, primary, its colors bathe the collision
        of the word & its sidereal double.
                (Mead notes this too).

The chapter gives no indication
        as to a progression of the Rays
                or the kathedra's final disposition
      after the brightness has abated.

                A footnote, possibly in her hand
            mentions a practice among certain Alexandrians
              of building altars from the bones
                    of the ibis.
But it does not say what they who built them hoped to shelter.

Ariel in the Marketplace

She is identified in the surviving texts
primarily through the recurrence of certain tropes:

>"wing"
>"library"
>"seed"

So a ghost weaving the prowl of her own voice
through the whirlwind of the
corpus symbolicum.

"Devotion" she says, is a [   ] (possibly two words)
& the light rescinds, [~~unbounded~~].

She strolls across the
morning of the great festival, the sea close beside her
& the Grand Corniche strewn with petals.

All day long she opens the single letter —
the book that wrote itself
                out of air, out of dust, from the heavy silt
of beach fires and washed up wood
                where the noise you hear is only
the names and counter-names
a confusion of precision rhymed with the dead.

The Book, O Prince, is a dream of one white letter.

First Letter to Iamblichus

Iamblichus, my darling, the insensate world throngs us
        we are grief in its floodrush to ruin.
                Who will take passage through
                        the doctrines of the Book
      gathering
the perfectible errors of our operations
                        miming disfigurement
        to assail resurrection?

(And who will come after us to burn
the ladder whose structure is motion, a dialogue of the one
& the none?)

Sovereign as lake water
        reed-tasseled, serene
the Countenance haunts my speech
                with the mirror of the true dying.
Not this demarcation, but its bitter writing
                      through
to unravel night by a theory
                of horror
& mend the negative with the other
                of history.

            (No pardon till first we walk the Tablets
      by a sequence of pure sound).

But I am owned of love and its law is a star
        a flame for ascending the spine of the lighthouse
            announcing the knot of each
                    syllable.

Alexandria, if you would mend the ghost
        be the author of a world.

Ariel on Canopus & The Signature

You will walk by the great river
        but it will not be a river.
You will say "now it is midnight"
        but it is only the star overhead.

Soma pneumatikon and then what?
(Lapse of doves, paleologos fade out —)

            The world lightless speechless sealess
                  worldless.

I cannot remember now what they looked like.

        Only this is real, my Master.
            Your strange technology
                for bringing back the dead
                      inside of a book.

You have to hear (what).
[The gnostic iron of the angel in her dress of sidereal cold]
        You have to hear
                whatever She will, even dead, mark upon the
tablet.
        (Sigil, rudder, tear)

(the One has grown lost in the soul of an animal)

& then her Messenger, Who came to us day after day with her Signature
(it lays glittering —)

She said (the candle poised above the pool in shadows):

Form poses the dead, is door & echo   through echo

(**a** minus All Ways).

Form, ignited
engulfs the body.
                      First by song.
  Then by Tremendum.

Poem for the Dismembering of the Poem

This is the gorgeous, the lame, the ruinous
planet of paradise falling
through rhyme as
      the speed of your voice
rushs the dysmorphic world
oiled apparatus grounding
      sugar
into dust.

It was never the true promise anyway, its winch
of blue fire aglow above
      evening's breakwater.
Rather the run of litter
out of which the free graves
      of sparrows are built.
From the dirt they still murmur their endearments.

Naïve messages about
invasions from the future
bombard the region of the brain
that governs pleasure.
                At zero hour commence
          the deletion of passwords.
The firewall shattered by
the malware of lyric

until the poem, too, is wholly dismembered.

The Spectral Logic of the Temporal Folds in on Itself

                she writes, so that
grammar becomes a parable about decay
        & how each book makes a shadow to
trail after it.

The Unwritten
                can only speak of hope
which is a wound we carry and learn to believe in.

But if I enter the broken world
tracing the visionary company of
departed love & trailing what starves
then only by its logic
        can I link
each ghost to its aura of dust.

Which is also a letter:
nocturnal hosannah, inhuman vesper.

To be concerned with grammar
is to take up utopia.

To take up utopia
is to consider the mechanism
by which it will
one day
burn us
to the ground.

The Poem of Fire
>for Teresa Villa-Ignacio

But this is the poem, alive and burning.
The poem of fire, in the quires of its turning.

This is the fire, this is its home
alive inside its burning of time

and this is the time of the poem's burning
alive yet dying in the smoke of its quotes.

This is the smoke that could be home
the whirling, the failing, this is the hope

and the hope of the smoke is for a fire
composed of nothing but quotes.

This is the quote, ignited by smoke.
The smoke of the poem that fuels the fire.

The word as it turns, chanting the end
and this is that spiral, the poem that is failing.

The smoke of a choir as it slowly wavers.
The hope of smoke inside a quote of fire.

To Be Two (Proleptic Seizure)
        for Ingrid

Or the fire of love is a letter from the king
        a seizure in the shape
        of a rose.
Where the will to possess must also
        erase you.
I am gone from this planet.
        Uplink datastream
        now.

Or the fire of love is the uncommon name
        La bella donna
        Che cotanto amavi.
Drawing distinct pressures along a line
        of invisible pleasure.
The force to wound to harrow to kiss.
        "The stones themselves are
        burning."

Or the fire of love remains exterior
        to language
        a Rose
In the garden of the Rose
gate of loaves & never.
No speaking of desire is valid without
        asking "How may I
touch you?"

Or the fire of love will streyne him by the herte —
al sodenly a-swowne
        in the whirligig of dream.
Server crash <unknown error>.
Re-boot erotic software

to find that a fool
& his transcendence
   are soon parted.

Or the fire of love alarms the world
   and its tongue into a great
   doxology.
That madrigal is most apt that will
   lift a white wing.
From skin to skin Wide Area Network
all a-swarm in ethercloud
   array my touch & gaze.

Or the fire of love goes haywire
a wayward nightingale
   devising the dervish
of syncope. In the hall of the archive the light of it
   lowers lips to a moan
and then. What measure will consecrate
   me as I am
gaudium resurrection?

Or say that the fire of love is
what cannot be
   contained.
"Those branches which were a-flame
   became red-rose trees."
If loosed then a wing
that cries
   inside a river.
How else will love astonish the hinge & poverty of living?

The Book of Drowning
        for Anna Deeney

Is the book where reading is séance.
                The eye flickers over
flickering letters
              white in their paper evening.

                        (A single letter saturates the eye)

If the soul is harmony, as Plato says,
then the scroll will be what
disturbs. Emerging from the archive
the way fire grows from
wood.

I am concerned with facts which may belong, says Ariel Breton,
to the order of the pure, but which present all the appearances
of a signal, without being able to say
which signal –

It is, therefore, not
the end of dreaming
                but another chapter
in the catalog of the pharmakon
                the one liquid with the promise
of lyric.

Other word for disaster.

Annals of the Tree of the House of Dust

To read the Book backwards
go blind along an hour
of descending blossoms
hold incendiary twilight
        (crown of desire)
hold
the monstrous hero who
performs epic infusion
sails to another shore
breaking the bright ring
of *nostos*
              for the sweat
of the beautiful instant
of loss & circumference.

Said Ariel:
"The sun who dwells and guts
— whose answer is an altar designed for emptiness
— the sea of a million *nella miseria*
            carry
the documents of my gaze
past bones & prayers

Speak
as I land at the kingdom
of the irreducible
gold filtered between green boughs.

For landing
is falling
& falling
a going beyond."

As the pawn sparrow
on a destitute branch is
the godly lodestar of spring
in its loneliness
        so the neural net-weave
        refolds
catastrophe inside
the ten nodes of the tree.

Who enters speech abolishes distance —
Brings us near, as near as breath —

Keter to Tiferet
the green grass
bends in the house of dreaming
elder sign of desired shore
oars dipped in white fuel
blades for the keening.

Smoke's Book

The smoke of the book after great labor
gives off a scent of evening.

It is sweet to read there among a confusion of letters
where a sparrow is also an Angel
        come down chanting
psalms for the unbearable
bell of a tulip
pitched one degree
beyond silence.

Say I read through the night and into whiteness
& say I am both ointment
        & a reef on fire
            a ship off the coast
& a scribe of the text's darkness
baring my arm, my face
        my entire work
to the unbearable sun.

Whoever would quench me
drowns in a glade of light &
whoever then reads me
bears limit
like a cup
for endless refilling.

Who writes me, rewrites me.
Makes a history of
care, marking all
my errors as eros.

Exact Presence
        after Yves Bonnefoy

"Exact presence whom no flame can ever again hold back"
        I turn in you as Thoth turns
communicating what I cannot as yet see
its governing wavelengths broadcast
        on the narrowest of bands
        its archangelic photons emanating
the discharge of hyperousia which is itself a black body
        form of radiation hovering
much as a ship hovers suspended above a crystal of pure water.

About you there is nothing at all exact because form
        grows forever multiple shadows
out of its shifting presence. They bewilder us, we are
aghast, shivering in the daydream between arches
        where the cold run of excession
        trembles in the zero
of its own regard — striking signals, silence
        the greater ward of that mission
to ignite the parables of a green earth inside mysterium tremendum.

Datacluster, netweave, neural fire bearer.
        Crow as dawn sips migrant
        toxins for the sundering
of a fever & the body of delirium, its wreckage
named I-burn-over-midnight & marked by whose hands?
        Instant of the supply
        harrowing my sister
her wild stare to afternoon another river or.
Is it the strange among us, inside us, chanting misery/pulchritude

Hosannah flare-dust in the afterglow?
        Ship of all degrees

point of wheeling light & a seizure of the left hand
in its sensorium canopy, come as far as the sound
        of bees over a field
        of grass & snow.
Revolve in your finitude as the form of longing
        over many years
traversing arc of skull, vibratory prayer & threshold.

Archive
        for John Drabinski

And then the small books
without witness.
Ghosts
patching history.

Wanting clairvoyance.
The othering toward
a new moored
shore.

Wanting lumens
at springtide
& the city singing
in green wheat.

Unspanned
surge of green
vowels.
Utopian chasm found.

Etude for the Monstrance of Nothing

And I reach the Book
        and it is broken into blossom.

        At the place
        where loss & structure
        become
the same thing.

        As a little bridge of grass
        is a late beginning
        to the stars.
Uttering the monstrance of summer.

But then to go beyond
        the white book
                seeing to the edge
                of the alphabet
        that is endless.

In the pages of the Book
the lost things
        are kept as lost.
Kindling for *parousia*
inside another word.

The enigma of memory is that it exceeds living.
More than I see I misremember.
                Swim minnows
                          through shadowed pool.
                                Swans
                  adrift on a river.

The long plunge

           to form is continual.
It is nothing, I say, nothing
                to fall into the Book
        or to pray without ceasing for the company of unknown names.

Summer in the Street of Cisterns

Because the vessels will never be able to contain
        the Abundance

the cascade of
        radiance that
        pours out from
        the breaking
of the Book
to cover the length of the street and overflow its dust
with dust.

Enter random search query:
              Semiotic whispers as
the algorithm for repletion.

    &&
the dawn gone to swanned rust —
    &&
the Sum of Hosannahs draining away —
    &&
the nakedness of speech
shedding its words
one by one.

By ruin I climb ruin.
The Book's catalog of sorrows
its emendations, its erasures.

Gazing out on what, after us, is
        a scripting of
        impossible flowers —

The Books of Remembering

      1.

In the spring, the city is full of gods.
They speak in the sun and the scent of absinthe leaves.

In the silver of the sea, the blue room of sky
in the whiteness of the streets, the trees alive with birds.

Here entire faiths arise out of words
for a king's disappearance.

Nocturnes for the gaze which singed us.
The rain-touch of fever that turns our friends to stars.

But to cross out the world
with the promise of a World?

It must come back to Song — lumens, love & the names
for the double-flicker of what resists & resurges.

"Maintaining the enigma
in the void of its answer"

means irradiating each splinter
in its stanza of wood.

My love, an archive is only
the d/ark in the moment of any speech.

2.

And how did they
burn the books?
They burned them
in each of their letters.

And how did they burn
the vowels and their worlds?
They burned them from domus
to cantus, from smoke to rune.

Did they burn the stations
of their discontaining?
In the house of smoke the ghost
of the book rises above the last ember.

A ghost is only a voice
exhuming disruption of desire
giving to negation
the persistence of hope.

Where the book turns wood
into flame and flame into emerald
there a wing gives I to I .
And there all the planets drop in the Sun.

Day unto day uttereth speech.
Where the twenty-six fragments
are burning in the brightness of foaling
each into each.

Lyrics for the Lost Book of Ariel
      for Tim Morton

"Corporeality is the goal of the ways of God" — Friedrich Schelling

      1.

It was Ariel who walked the blue shards
And spelled the ligature of the fall and its foaling.
Ariel who beheld the ruin of the body
In the body's morph and prism.

The gulf of days was a bell and its echo
Calling across the bones of the sea.
Ariel sang beyond every genius
And she was burning as she came.

Like a glass poured into a river
She unbequeathed all signatures.
The star that hung its light for her eyes
Crowned her hair with the sign for abandon.

O come by wand, by cup, by nothing.
Like a halo, like a flicker, like a bomb.
Who will release the melligenous song
Of the last of the day that discompletes us?

Or say the instant of this shattering
Deletes the running of form and becoming.
Say she is nowhere but the frame of dissolving
And we are the wreckage of her bourne and her wake.

2.

Ariel says:
the dance is
of a world gone
to the edge of its
own light.

She says:
the ode and what
breaks it
measure the same
thing.

3.

Ariel broke the book in two.
The sentence inside spoke,
it said:

Language comes as a sign beyond all others.
The of-itself reaching out to another.

Like love, its energy pervades
all that it touches.

It cannot hold enough.
It is here and over. Endless.

4.

Lyric, says Ariel, is the barcode of the dead.
It mourns us into dreaming.

But to be given over to the other
is as smoke from an arrow

or music out of a goblet of apples
when all the guests have gone home.

      5.

Ariel murmurs thalassa
not as Xenophon did
but for the dove whose light singes
all who see it.
The dove is requisite
a burning into time.
Its wings are shadows
inside a white fire.

The mother of the dove
is the earth in its turning
saying we cannot
not praise our own becoming.

The hard thing is to be awake
under stars nor to drown
their sparks in a flood of words —
dream-specter in the chorus of hooded glory.

The issue of tears is the great form of desire.

      6.

Ariel drinks and says:
The night in which all cows are black
is only the sweetness of a form unseen.

She does not enter as the answer
to your poem.

Wine and the darkness of day descend.

    7.

Grass is a crown, she says, it goes beyond bitterness.
It makes the bones of the sea satellite, radiant.

Ariel burns in her dress and she burns supine
and she says (she says) I will be your idol.

    8.

Ariel says:
the Pure Land is a fragrance
& a breath I learn to say
& unsay.

The stain of the body
grows its crystal — involution
mounting to a height
unguessed.

A clod of clay
that deepens each day.

It spreads out across the four worlds.

9.

To shed the doctrine of the Blind
you must first go by way of the unseeing.
Holy is the night in which all cows are black,
by which occlusion narrows the focus to a single bead.

The vision of a dawn hangs by a thread.
To see me by the grain I am & uttered whole
enter through the sound of bells.
The brightness of the scission enfloods the eye.

Or else the hood of glory is a singing also
in the narrowness of the body's prism.
Become what bleeds away, what casts
its flare to the shore of thigh & finger.

The ultimate of Wheels rolls in gold and stutters
as the farness of the sundered comes
to hold us in a tide of revolving lights.
Gaudy Ariel, the rapture encants us one cell a time.

The Dream of Yeats

And the women who burned
Shelley's body

did they burn the book of shadow
& all its letters?

Did they write their names
as music sliding out of sleep

& strewn with broken figures?
Were their heads circled with light?

Being dead, did they rise
as swans and so create

the final reach to
translunar paradise?

Because I speak death joins
joy to the intercourse of light.

The soul in the evening walks
beside my love. The soul is a song

that forms the body with a look.
Now an apple cups its poise of dew

and all the grass is gone to shivers.
Death, ruin Earth, then go past ruin.

But an apple for my true love, who walks
through evening, the green stain of its furnace.

The soul is what they say
cannot stop from singing.

Grass, what goes through Avalon
ravenous, its cold green water running.

H.D. in Egypt

So it was nothing, nothing at all
the first words that found me
perfecting the Mysteries

as a circlet may break
in the heat of the poem's fire
and a boat carry the beloved

to the place where we read by starlight.
My sign-posts are not yours
but may my words help you, traveler

as you cross this uncertain land.
The darkness is only archive,
the spirit of the Book that keeps us.

Alive in its promise we see the reach
of earth extending, the body of light
become the body of flesh

the signal speaking the whorls
of poesis, the madness of the world
falling down around our ears.

I do not remember the prayer or command.
I no longer can recall what the Message said.
All I know now is carried in song —

that we must burn as we live
ignited of Ship, and croon and sway,
and never forget.

Theurgical Etude for Nate Mackey

The song, spun, and
at the end of it, un-
      done.
As the archive,
      its pages in ruin
rewrites the myth
of its own demise
      abides
in it, the flat
octaves mounting
      to the sky.

Undone,
as music
bleeds in the wide
eyes of the Bride.

The steps she climbs
so so, so swift, as
      certain as tide
      & tide falls

with the rumor of
      a ruin of time –
so her steps, re-paced,
      measure the bright
      stairs, in
stars of cadence,
      each
a prayer, the whole
song of it splayed
         & broken
      re-opened

to the page of white
        letters,
each letter
        begetting

a further begetting
        & from the ruin –
this song, done, at
        the end of it,
                not done.

Thought's Smoke
       for Teresa Villa-Ignacio

So I was thought, she
thinks (not thinking)

So I was spoke, she
says (not spoken)

and the day room
swept by a full

moon and the curtain
unharmed by a breeze

it is autumn
someone said —

under the leaves
and the moon lies under

autumn, she
murmured, who

will be the last
to sit down

to table & speak
as speech that is smoke

leaks out who will hold out
hope for the ghosts

that they sweeten the meal
or be the first

to come out and look
as the moon falls through the west

as it slides, as it goes
under the leaves?

Gnostic Frequencies

Imagine this, murmur as murmur only just
this much of white's whiteness
giving body color. Cold the blue eyes
now the white insists it grows older
together but never what it is imagine this.

Imagine this, murmur. Color and no body.
Color and no bird fixes the light of its song to a branch.
Color and not all white. As murmurs, as pulses.
Feeling the séance of matter as it leaks through the hands.

Imagine this, murmur.
The epochal and the apocryphal.
The dune shifting and the planet lying low tonight
under stars the cars drift westward and the cars
are in heaven and driven by angels.

Imagine this, murmur.
For it is night. Your speech is low.
It is the door and the window. It says
to go out is not to spread a name
but be host to the power of what is in between.

Murmur, imagine this.
Only shining white infinite but not known.
In its heat a sentence murmurs
the secret of transparency is
the opacity of its halo.
Light over all. Light falling through
the graphs of light that are silent and on fire.

Imagine this.

Tremble
>for Anne Waldman and Ed Bowes

Trembling from the trembling of the other
and trembling with the trembling of desire
for what cannot come as satisfaction
what goes beyond the longing for it
except in calling out the body shivers
there is no other answer except to move
in the love of whatever comes and unseals us.
Valve as the pressure to go under moan
>or utter wave & sever.

For the annulling of self is necessity
and by it the separate hinges move
in oils of speech & petals. Infinite alteration
beckons from the street or window.
Desire is the truth of desire as neither self nor
what self reaches. To be precisely other
in the vowel of this description means there is
no other utterance for by desire we are never
>ended & what you gave glows yet.

But as the world is a waking to the other
who arrives and carries in a look what
uncovers me to my self, so I am witness
to the long loosening of the tremble, to its
rain-drenched, gold-planished crossing
of a wing with a branch. Inside such giving
is a becoming again out of lack. And desire
is the strophe. To send & replenish the other
>who trembles, in a river, always comes back.

In a Somer Seson

Of fire to fire renew
summer the fall
of light and season
of mortal dews.

Overall the evening
set of moon
August high in the trees
equatorial burn.

Grass under green water
& cycle of song
in circle renew
fire of summer to summon

Or signal the fade
of the long moon that burns.
Orbit of fire alive
under green water too.

Envoi

And then of wind
        strewn in arcs
what wind, I said, could graft
        light to wood?

Strum of thorn
        in bones
& amen moan the rosaries
        of the stylus.

Given length of water
        its westness
all lights founder.
        Shone down on us

splinters & hazards.
        Canopian watch-fire
for the wilderness
        of words.

from *Song X*

Ode to Song X

Whoever croons it, feeds
    it — steps it down
through coal
    reblazes it.

Wonder, blank water
    & whoever pours it
    summons ghosts
in a flutter of sails.
    The noise of séance
thrumming through mud & river.

A river is what slushes crud
    into spirit.
Whoever craves the crux
    of song must
turn oxygen into
    forgiveness

    writing over tabula
errata in a fever
    of fine print
as the echoes of migrant
    voices drift
up the well of song
    looming bluer
than zero.

Song X (on form)

Song X?
   Whatever goes beyond the end.
Past conclusion's rumor of
ruin, through the blank
gutters of margins &
   into the sweet space
sweeping over
the bare ground
dreaming down
   to zero.

If it is whiteness
then it is whiteness
unwritten.

A flare of tissue
   in a black glove
a glove stained by grey ash
   a song
murmuring O
   marking its
X in the white
sand.

As windfall, caritas.
   The poorness of form
peering into
   the abyss.

So that maybe it begins again.

Summer as a Theory of Song X

Because I was White Flower, throat lozenge
        "the ultimate thing"
procuring guitar solos
across venetian bridges.

Because
this is the beauty that smites the city
        folds up, intricate with
song's invasions.

"It is white, not quite white" – the history of
repose, untitled, in the midst of losing faith
        its jet falling through
a long blue climb

and rumors
of flooded lands
and the life to come
that is the same as this one.

Whoever I was I was
mild as whiskey and murmuring the summer
as summer, noon into fire through the cool
flue of evening.

Is the stars folded up and the ruined land
        where you go
walking the marketplace
        squinting as glass
stabs the heart
and is never finished.

Number 9 Dream

And in this series—it leads to
another, the changes
for migrating
cross the lawn with the moon
dividing, then subdividing.

Lip synching caesura.

It grows clustered. Ferns, birds
the weather above
the harbor, even the waves
accede to the vast
continual remittance.

The way a guitar remembers Sunday.

Brief palsy.
The bricks burned ochre for an hour.
Seized by the strangeness of
evening you would dream she
drowns, and you drown, too.

Sundown, or another name for it.

Aesthetic Theory
for Tim Bahti

The dead are the stones and the stars speaking all night. They watch us in our sleep, rub oil into our hair, press feathers to our eyes. The mote of light in the glass of water. The place (the motion) where each name offers to another what is severed.

To be dead is not a clearing, but a confusion with no end to the echoes, a plunge through the infantile neologies of the world and the speech of everyone who suffers. A prayer to silence to find the one word that will float.

Wood good for a boat. White swan, summer smoke.

The beautiful is a kind of noise we love.

Song X *(neither dream nor actual)*

Whether of the mind or actual, the tranced movements of a woman waving amen and from a street sign one capital letter to give hope its aureole.

Blue train of twilight flicking sparks in the wind & silent reading in the lighted rooms of buses. The secret promise of grammar murmuring Polis is this: the speed of a song rushing ahead for the dead who go on needing their shoes and their books.

Twilight, a crowd moving, and in each puddle the glitter of forensic runes. To walk through the city you must cross those spaces lit by nothing but images.

Drive all night through empty streets, confusing the words for harbor and desert. Come to the edge where the edge bleeds off, the syllable lies motionless in the grass.

Dream of Song X

In another dark
to move as they do –
caesared with wind
sonic because of
bloom.

And then
disrailed – the catenary
thrill inside
the company
of the mute.

Wherever the sun,
no, wherever
a finger moves its
chalk through
the dust.

Caverned and patterned.
Diced out of hold.
No particular but this
star blotched white
so soon and yes.

As if were waiting.
Because the
waiting. Seven or
sun up. The same odes
of azure.

Something else, then.
The vitamins, the blue
fall of epic. A

windows' delirium. Leaf
splay late afternoon.

A word is happenstance.

Song X as Final Etude

If the soul could —
If the soul were butter
or if the soul were dirt
it could see you better

and then where on earth
to take the spoon from sorrow?

If the drift were bigger
the weight of it, hefted —
If the slow ink of its death
dropped clear the way

then bells, after.

If the ride to the station
in winter, at night —
if the night blazed carillons
then how we'd want to

want to be bitter –
Glory of stars saying under stars.
The saying of stars is litter.

Then the soul dives —
Then the soul all under
its coat of shivers shivers —

Giving Account

So I try to begin a story about myself. Will there be images? Is that a poem? Or is it narrative? What is a narrative? A series of links? Is that what a poem is? A sequence for binding a ritualized self. But this is not a self. This is a text.

And then where is the song, someone asks. Who gives it melody? Is it for grief or wonder? If I am to be I, then a structure ensues. Observe the rules for disclosure and elision. Someone says "witness this." Winter, Wednesday, or next.

I try to begin a story about myself, but it becomes a story about a boat and a dollar. The boat is a dove and the dollar is on fire.

What is the word for being together and what is the word for remnant?

But what is the sentence for love, love?

What is the word for give?

In Memory of My Nostalgia
       for Luke Menand

"You have to be your own sorrow king."
Raining in the trauma of daylight
& the paleness that the poem, now mis-
guided, disarticulates across every
        antecedent.
You have to be—unbequeathed.
    More than
displaced, but something a little less
than wholly exiled, rooted to the kingdom
      of a subway seat
the stump of a soggy book.
You have to love the welter of loss
rhyming the cantilevered structures of
belonging with an off-the-wall
     rimshot.
              I shouldn't be
telling you this, but even this poem is an effort
to further future suffering and solely by sound
propagate new wounds. That cut into
a city street, exposing a
hidden warren, the theologies
of undisciplined happiness/
     Stupid, right?
           But then to soak in
the green, skimming the tranced
scenographies of a secular spring.
    Page after page
        in the museum of light —
Irresistible.
     We can gulp the air, skirt
the skirts, make of the dismal pastime
of an afternoon a Brownian drift of

        motes in their gold-
           fall lounge act.
Like that time (the first time) you saw
everything, forever—& a radio drowned
          you in a song.
Your soul's appetite fell, carnal
on the carousel of a spurious kiss.
Which persists, in the desire for
        a single inad-
           missible wish.

The Dream of Perfectible Capital

This is the story of our longing. Where the city communes with itself. Rising, it grows strong inside the dream of perfectible capital.

This is the house of glass. The place where the living meet their ghosts. Cake is served. The florettes of the interior are beyond count. They bid you enter wonder and breathe as a toy would breathe, in a landscape of inviolable nearness.

Saturated by sugar, gazing out, two by two, at the white horizon.

>   White beyond white.

>   A star that drowns the eye.

Star Dot Star

So to be of another color you say I must subdue the cold. Furnish it with a lantern hung in frost, under a sky whose contusions are the hue of blueberry juice staining the white porcelain spaces no how.

Much like the hereafter, winter scatters diamonds through the void. A plane goes down behind a hill. The bodies of the passengers languid as fumes from a glass of whiskey.

Oh, I see the fawn that lays its head on the colorless page. It trembles, because everything's included. Ideas of heaven. The monstrosity of living. Your face, my love. Star dot star.

Dianoia

Narrative details might form
a ballad about a princess
or any handsome young woman
who would fain lie down.
But to classify the subject
by meters, focusing on
a catastrophic moment,
would also signal the typical
betrayal and elevation
of a TV loneliness
as attested to by
the attendance of crowds
and the spectacle of roses
and signatures, which are all
we have really, when you come
down to it.
                    Of a loveliness that daily
fed us nothing is certain
but the crisis of its aftermath.
It involves images of dearness,
repeated many times over.
Kissing the wounds that were so red.
A species of deer distinguished
by a supernal color
so that its gawky movements,
fabricated as they are,
give us a sense that an increase
in the amount of available light
is what lends consumerism its tragic tone,
the *lieux de memoire* of
the lost participatory dimension.

The Idea of Evening as Abode

Is it how we gather then at the edge
of belonging and each humming
the twilight music she knows
best? The land is empty
and the sound of its distances
pushes into view the idea
of evening, the long
force of diminishments.

The lake is an instance of coming
into reception's other mode.
The pain of its placidity a melting at the tip
of sight, strained so in its plain
of smooth blank fire and under,
what is that? except the name
for the tone the body gives
off when it lapses
and the name is all
that is left.

      Fire, banked
exhalation, deep roll of
the cloud all light and plunging
to bled blue. You want a place
that is the name of your belonging
a sequence for the grass
beneath stars, the hard
passing of it.
           Want
a flame so that encloses
you to the last and is span
for the pulse and ring
of the still-listening-bells

their thermal updraft
psalmic gate,
water shed for
the transmission of the whisper
the king who said it
and his chair is this falling
through the altar
the ground that
undescribes you.

The Real Real

Whoever sees the real charges the eye with a flare.
Keeps evening kneeling, a blue-smoked air
stripped of its string of lights
given as the park to the people
and where they move there,
from path to path, each node cinched and fluid,
the cold edge of a run over ice
to where the middle is a bridge
and not anything separate.
The weather for it melting, I mean the way
it's built out of the ground and because of it
a shelf is what it says will last,
will hoist the fables of the margin
even after the spire is misrepaired.

The Lover's Dictionary
for Jen Jahner & Chris Hunter

Without vocabulary, the heart drowns.
Yet what we love is any instance
of inarticulate speech raised up
inside of zero and glowing alone in its halo.
It makes from the face a sonnet
of imperfect grammar.
It gathers us in luminous embrace
and from an ark of bone builds its radiance
spilling over desk lamps, bookshelves
streetcars, roof tiles, palm trees
your hair in the wind
the brightness of your voice calling
all things in that flood rush to the page
to be touched with miraculous nearness.

Theory of Shelter

A man is all stealth.
Listening does him in.

To move by excess is what
he means by living.

A man is a knife and the road
he walks on cuts two ways.

Communication by lamplight
is a gesture toward infinity.

The day is a rant.
All fecklessness and high tide.

In Mandelbrot's "entity of infinite resolution"
the demands for clarity grow unbearable.

A man is an entity with a gesture
toward resolution.

To be weary is what the living mean by it.
To cede it. Discontained.

Communication in a park with lamps
configures a nostalgia for infinity.

A man is a system of leaves and shadows.
He finds under lamplight a stone alone.

Near Midnight

Of the inexplicable
        that is the other side of speaking
the void and what saves us
        into folly
                a radiance
        that pains like
                a movie star's red satin
        her deep carnivorous smile.
Who burns, who longs, who slips away like thunder

The one tender thing
        to do
by which I name my bridge, you
                    October come the gates and mourning
by whose direction
        do we fall
                    towards earth
the desert where the star turns its light
                        to the space of home
                            is a small fire.

Is a small fire kindling with
            bones of saints
            the sunken boats for the dead
            who call to us from song.

Or I am so small the tree upholds me
        in its sleep, a surge kept to a music inside the palm
            the minute hand
                sending grace-notes
                    of fading.

That will utter me as glass
                as water flowing over slate.
Molten, a potion
                in the king's eye
                              adoring.

Poem Beginning with a Line by Hugh Seidman

As if the human had marred the human, or
else married it, we said.
As if the emblem for belonging still gleamed
visible, a sign of wealth, a puddle of light
at the base of your throat
and the music distilled because that is the verb
the ghost of the poor can carry us no farther.

To give up oblation is to render judgment.
The scissored, the granite, the oblique words
for exequy – shivery as paper or elm leaves.
Whoever knelt, slid to wet pavement, spoke exodus
in a bastard rhyme to implore the lost
and ask them to be taken up as chosen.
Seven sentences. Unfolded time.

Inside, it was water. It was quiet and not whole
but the skin gave off a light and you were there
beside us, on astral wavelengths, requited
not requited. The perfect lens we hoped would
cure us blurred over by the cataract of séance.
This proverb does not mend.
The whole point of inside is to burn

And not begin. Or begin, as she who promises
tulips by the window and a cup of tea.
As spring envelops flesh and bends to drink again.
This morning morning's minion flew up in snow
& rumors of bad amen.
The haunt of comic book apotheosis.
Now the good enough rain descends.

We should go so afraid.
Keeping the dark to our skin and the singular
trade in ruin spelling the only work of the living.
For the dead gorge the glory of their exit
with empty lines, the sublime at the signal-limit.
It is said they do more than remember.
It is said they will pour out their signals of distress forever.

Three Songs for the End of the World

1.

Or is it evening already?

Then slip becalmed into sleep.
Lie extinguished at the wick.

Because we never fully arrive
at the figure where we are named
but go to market darker.

2.

If a form grows visible
at the edge of the body's
thrumming
it must come as liturgy.

Continual oblation and melting
inside day's long signal flare.

More sun than paraclete.

More water than hosannah.

3.

To build an arch over sound made out of sound.

To enfold the brightness of earth
within the lower octaves
of a trembling.

Speak memory
the five dolorous wounds
of belonging.

Lallation for dust, inside of dust.

Ground gone over & wept.

Heat Death
        after DeLillo/for Jeremy Green

Because heat collapses
through a tube, one atom at a time.
Because it instigates rumors
of dry land and tables heaped with burnt fruit.

        In the terrible parable of verticality
        the body shimmers till it dissolves.

Because ancient heat
braids its information at the tip of
plutonic metal.

        Is saturant, exfoliant,
        a blister at the cusp of Sumerian twilight.

That we are burned along a line
of pomegranates and hairshirts.

Just as earth could burn.
As if earth were already cinder & cone.
As if sky were no longer sky.
This is the logic.

Because heat is a balm
& a treasure and in its mouth
the lozenge of the Body
        dissolves.

O you who are passing green
through all your days
dissolve before the equation
and mount to the sun your requiem of pearls.

Incendiary gleam.
Radium shantih.

Pluto to the last of sun.
Bomb all over this world.

The Idea of Limit (9/11)

But the higher error
of the stars
is how light has been
spilt

split
into further
light

The excellence of the fall being so great
it is what the bitter call nostalgia

    *

Stood
at the edge of edges
looked out saw
the burning

the human
severed
             by the human

the fragility
    of the absolute

    *

Graced
    by mere mention of grace

Going by moaning
not meaning

what could be
could be the
stutter of amen

   *

The angel appeared among the ruins.
He said, this is the sign of X.
Wash your hands
    with it.

Coming of Age in the House of Dust

And so I am slaved
to the outermost rim of the wheel
server-to-client
typing and re-typing the password
        for seizure.

        But in the gathering shadow of electrical storm
        white chairs lay lit by the not-yet.
        A longing comes to disappear inside grass.
        If lightning is caused by wind trapped in a cloud, writes Lucretius,
        then please see me as I stand here
        in my rain-cloak of shadow
        in the beauty of the elementary held as a flicker
        in the white feather of matter.

In the House of Dust a fever
        and a name for it.
The wall of the heart slides back
        to reveal
o\sonograms of infinite
        remorse code
beside a small care for what remains.

Bring to earth things of the body.
Their ache for touch
        soft sift
        and a candle.

Except it water the planet
        and give
brilliance to the waves
the movement
of the human
        comes in vain

the richness of my father at sea is a stone

lovely he makes the ship be blue
blue-fingered its sternum, too
in the quiet after
the doctor has left the room.

The richness of my father all at sea
is a ship that tows a stone and a long
dropping to shadow though bright
he fell through a house-dark well.

Folded, he says the least
feather calls out prayer.
And could I ablute him
then I'd refute the oriole and its shiver.

The richness of my father all at sea so poor
is a dropping into blindness
his de-lanterned throne
the debt we eat from

salt thrown through a window.
The strangeness of the hereafter
a morning in a roll call
of chains that are chains of coal.

My stone is my work, he sings
my sternum the urge for a fast blue ship.
The richness of a planet a useless seizure.
The sunrise is for dogs to piss on roses.

The Tears of Things
for my father, Frank Pritchett

A man lives in a room. Goes out to burn his days.
Stumbles at the threshold.
Winnowed. Fissured.
A passenger who frames his story
as the outlandish one about the wayward.

Inside a stone, they say, is a tear.
Inside the scattered papers on the desk
and inside the sentences and inside
the insistent wind that is whiter than the trees in winter.
We will meet there and give our prayers to the gravel.

What does a pronoun have to do with a life
and how will we stay at the edge of sunlight
that takes everything under it hostage?
This is what it means to say, you are not here.
Here, in the midst of everything

dissolved, but still the house and its rooms
carry your face and what you did day to day
is how you remain silently, in old woods
and irons, in worn out grips. In ancient, accurate swings.

Before there was sky and before there was knowing
and how did I know you when I was the one
entering the tears of my own face and seeing with my eyes
the fraught exhausted grace of sand blown across a patio.

The carrier of fire is one with the moon.
The moon which says each thing must tear itself wide open.
So that a hole abides. Central to what is living.
So that the objects that surround us gaze

right through us. As though we were clear of stain.
As though we were cured.

Ballad
      for my mother, Betty Pritchett

The day is a wheel.
How does it turn?

Like a sun, like a circle.
Like a circle that burns.

O the day is the distance
between love & the night.

It straddles the body.
It dissolves its own light.

A wheel, a gathering.
A looseness, a shattering.

Whatever runs toward itself
before plunging to black.

Because O is the distance
between love and its sign.

And now the vowel
of total circumference.

Who hushes the moon?
Who weeps the sun?

Or lays her down with a will
saying hope for "zero."

What was the name?
How did we say it?

Did we run to sundown?
Sing "house" for "loss"?

The day is a wheel.
Like a circle, it burns.

Deixis

This isn't the poem
that will remember you.
Empty of grace
it cannot place

you in your names
now nearly lost
to the silence of their own page
that is white going whiter.

What stays is waste.
November in its steel cage
a moon marooned
in stellar ice.

How do we think
we will look to
each other now
that this world

is abandoned
and the cold leaves
down can rain?
Sparrows scavenge

the dirt in song.
They cover
the garden with
the garden's ruin.

The Empty Room
after Hopper

Who we are, what we did there.
Where we stood
in the empty room
the sunlight streaming in.

What came before us
then left again.
Into whose morning do we
come over and over again?

And there is nothing there
but the sun
ample and simple
and bright on the river as the thought

that you are not here.
There is no duration. Only
speak of what remains
of what is left.

How nothing gives
so much back.
So many green leaves breaking
out from every empty branch.

Cadence

They say in words
how death is clear
a song like a wave
a wave made from song.

How no one defeats
song but the sound
of it holds
until it dissolves

yet is not lost from
the world nor is
the world lost
ever held but

by a song till the song
sings in a wave
and holds. A wave of
song that does not dissolve.

The Ossuaries of Snow

That they were trembling
in their breathing at the edge of
mere appearance or else dissolving
as salt dissolves in a glass of water.

That it was snow and it was burning
as it fell as it was drifting.
Escarpment at the blind
edge and then go under.

Meaning through erasure
they crown a hill
& send a shiver
through a wall of bodies.

Light off a pocked wheel rim
light rewriting light
a séance by the last bone
before it slips into the code of shadows.

What keeps pouring out is blue
and blue bereaves the city.
Who knows how
anything returns?

Grand Hotel Abyss

It is best visited in autumn
when the logic of the day
yields to the logic of the night.

Along the long road going north
it looks out over the sea's
extravagance

an island where the light of exile
drifts through the open window.

Then the guest rises from the piano
gestures over his cocktail
speaking as a lover speaks

of the séance that is time
and the slow dissolve to the not-yet.

The question of movement, he says, is
first predicament.

"Can the real be the thing continuing
and not its broken light?

The tree of perfect noise
burns inside its signal."

Past the balcony's edge
rain transmits a shower of leaves
and the abyss of birds

swirls wildly, their blind bodies
flying naked
in the wind

each throat crushing
the sphere of a perfect note.

Homage to the Raven
        i.m. Anselm Hollo

"And now what time is it"?
asks the raven at the end
of the world.

"Time to get with the program."

Here on planet Earth
the program demands
we transmit every message
through the fraying vocab
for belonging.

But look, says the raven.
I, too, am frayed.
Fading into the inky
blackness of my wings
where song is a structure
for the ruins of time
        my croak a kind of white
        melody ascendant
the spiral glyph of M31
        its arms of light
a cosmic call sign
        flashing
plenitude
        & emptiness.

"Like Marx or Helen's ankles
at the gates of dusk"
quoth the raven.

Adios, all you "guests of space"

soon to be remanded
to an infinity of un-
troubled dust.

But my poems refuse
to get with the program.
They will destroy
entropy forever.

Six Gnostic Songs

    1.

Then the shapes they found they sifted from shadows.
Crowned them with antique mirrors and stripped
each moon of its craters. They stripped the name from the town
and nailed it to its neon outskirts. Shaped the silence of space
till it loomed through the windows as window.

They shaped the color of horses and the road they were running down.
Rehearsed solitude with an aching for decibels.
They came to the end and swung around.
The end was not the end, but further down.

They shaped the lake at dawn, watched the satellite
trace its biblical arc. They swore it was fire
and tore up their poems. They wrote new poems on the graves
of the dead and the words were stolen and the names
of their authors eternal and burning.

    2.

Then they walked through the city
crossing bridges, smoking over cups of black coffee
enfilading a single hour with a song in the key of X.

They loved the bricks only after sunlight had left it.

They bustled among the Egyptian tropes of the afterlife
the boat of Ra, the tomb of Kum, and spoke of Billie
singing "A Sailboat in the Moonlight."

They went to Michigan, or Indiana, and held a trance in the alien corn.
They got to Chicago and bowed low before Gehry's titanium knot
that is the war bonnet of the Empire.

    3.

In the end the daughter found the daughter, entering through doors of
    water.

In the end all the daughters are the sadness of their fathers
as they pass through fire. They go to an island of companions
alive in the moment of singing and wait inside the rubble
under the arc lamp of noon for no one.

In the end what it means to be the daughter is to be awake inside the
    dream.
Conscious of being and conscious of dreaming.
To be fully wide awake inside the poem as it is dreaming.

    4.

I see me standing in a series of lights
at street corners, under desk lamps
in the dimness of mythic shadows
fingering the fine forensic tools.

I see me standing in a pool of things
lit from within and the song
they murmur is the song of X
that is drowning with them even where I stand.

I see me standing at the corner of St. Joseph and Jewell.
At the corner of Sunset and Gower. Whitsett and
Moorpark. At the corner of Iris and Folsom. At the corner
of Concord and Garden. At the corner of.

In the asterisk that occludes or names each event.
History, or erasure. The hymn of the tissue of fire
that Newton and Isaiah dreamt of.

Tissue of fire that breaches the world with its
nothing burning down to zero. Shiver of motion
in a room that is empty and afterwards emptier still.

    5.

And it is light. Light still.
Triumphant. Holding. Light
above the harbor. Light inside
the glass. A long light laid
along a string and what runs
that string is light.

And it is light and nothing
but light. God spoke the
light. But first he had need
of the darkness. First he had
need of the emptiness.
He had need of the nothing
and all it was filled with.
Nothing spoke the light.

And it is light and still light.
Nothing but light abounds.
Surrounds us. Becomes us.
As our sheets as our clothes.
As day and all its windows.
The blankness of glass that reflects only sky.

And it is light & we are moving
through it. Divining then slurring
our words. The depth of light
is a kind of darkness. The depth
of light is where
we build the capital of ruins.

      6.

A catena of words, letting other words in.
The abrupt, the unrealized. The crude, the imperfect.
The pure and the stupid. The moon of X.
Whatever I become. The moon that is smoking
over the Cambridge Savings and Loan.

A catena of words, he said.
The word for splendor joined to the word
for dirt. The hymn of Isaiah and the equation of Isaac.

A catena of words. Running through all the books.
Their fugue of pages Dead and still dreaming.
Held to the unforgiving words. Held to their promise.

The Death of The Author
for Jane Gallop

If I were a writer, and dead, then how bright the sky at evening when evening is a word for making other words.

And how I would love to be dispersed across the sky, ashes thrown to the wind and someone's beautiful eyes reducing me to a few precious details. Travelling outside whatever my life had been, joining me to a future that cannot know me, except as a toy that resurrects the destroyed.

If I were a writer and no longer a part of my story, but given over unseen to the birds at evensong, returning to the same life, the very same and yet different. Speaking warmly with strangers at the gate, skirting the paths through the park, spying on the couples who are kissing in their sleep, a part of the larger night where everything has already happened without me.

If I were a writer, and dead, I would enter the room of sudden desires. The one with salty foods and glasses of whiskey. The book there where I had left it. Your eyes, your voice.

Whatever pierces me. Speeches me. Even now, dead, writes me.

The Dream of the Poem
for Raul Zurita & Anna Deeny

In the boat of the dream we row
toward the world's end.
That is a waterfall where islands float
and gulls slice the light, the kind
only seen by the dead.
Like the movies everything's in color.
There's a kid in a red jersey
a kid on a bike pedaling furiously to stay alive.
And Ave Maria, who stands so close
he doesn't even know she shelters
his hopes as they drown in pockets
of useless money.
If poverty is a kind of heresy,
then all the poets are heretics, numbered zero.
The sign of the true faith that burns on
after language has been ground down to
nothing, the single truth that music knows.
In the dream of the poem
Liszt's sonnet for Petrarch
aches through its doleful chords.
Paradise is to shiver as their sliver enters
rays from a prism that pierces
the stone of hubris with forgiveness.
The voice of the dream says this is real.
"To live here is to live. There is no difference."

Dante or, The End of Poetry
       for Raul Zurita

And he stirred his coffee, the old poet, and spoke of Dante, and how Homer's journey to the underworld wove a thread through Virgil to the *selva oscura*. And that the *Commedia* was not to apex of Christianity, but its finale. That the enormous architecture of the poem was not built to house theology, but to protect man from the absence of God, who had already disappeared.

He said the beauty of Dante was in the flow of the rhymes, so subtle you did not even notice them. They flow like the water of speech and not even Spanish can capture them.

The old poet spoke slowly. As if feeling the weight of each word, its monumental heft. Its slippery lightness. And we talked of the work of poetry. Of how to revive the flicker of logos, its small fire, in a world where only a few fallen sparks persist.

And he said: we are at the end of poetry. Because a word is no longer a word, an image is no longer an image, and this has killed God.

He said, "I have tried to write Paradise."